PRINCIPLES OF THE PROJECT

STRATEGIES FOR EFFECTIVE COACHING AND MENTORING

PHIL BLACK

Author, Mentor, and Founder of The Manhood Project

Phil Black is an Author, Inspirational Speaker, and the Founder of The Manhood Project (TMP). The Manhood Project is a coaching and personal development program designed to maximize the positive qualities of young men, while minimizing their temptations to engage in at-risk behavior. The program focuses on character building, development of communication skills, and personal exploration.

Like many young men, Phil was raised in a single-parent home by his mother. Though she did everything a child could hope for in raising him, the absence of his father left more questions than answers as he searched for guidance while becoming a man. Over the years, Phil faced countless emotional and physical challenges. On September 27th in 1997, he nearly lost his life to an act of gun violence. That incident changed Phil's life forever and in many ways, became the driving force behind his work today.

Prior to creating TMP, Phil worked with an internationally recognized, education based nonprofit called City Year, LLC. There, he was able to use his background in Learning & Development to enhance staff and volunteer performance. Phil has also served as a Senior Program Manager, Learning & Development Expert, and National Sales Trainer. Phil's most recent position has been a lead trainer with PEAR (Program in Education and Resilience), helping him accrue more than a decade of experience in youth training.

In addition to his work with TMP, Phil (or "Coach Black") holds dual certifications as a Life Strategies Coach and Youth Leadership Coach. Phil is a member of the BMe Community, founded by Trabian Shorters (formerly of the Knight Foundation), and is a member of the Detroit City Council's Task Force on Black Male Engagement.

Past awards and recognition include: the Omega Psi Phi Fraternity Inc. Uplift Award for Community Service, Citizen of the Year Award from Clark Preparatory Academy, the 2013 BMe Community Leadership Award, Two time Spirit of Detroit Award recipient, the 2015 Torch of Wisdom Award winner for Scholarship, and his latest accomplishment- the recipient of the Presidential Award for Service.

PRINCIPLES OF THE PROJECT
STRATEGIES FOR EFFECTIVE COACHING AND MENTORING

Copyright © 2016 by Phil Black

Phil Black
2051 Rosa Parks Boulevard
Suite 1B
Detroit, Michigan 48216
www.tmpmentoring.com

Printed in the United States of America

Publisher's Cataloging-in-Publication data
Black, Phil
Principles of the Project: Strategies for Effective Coaching and Mentorship / Phil Black; with major contributions by Celeste Davis. Cover photo by Tim Paule.
p. cm.
ISBN 978-0-9979817-1-1
1. Education —History —Other category. 2. Another subject Social Science—From one perspective. 3. More categories —
HF0000.A0 A00 2010

DEDICATION

I dedicate this book to every individual who has the heart and mind to build others. Anyone can share knowledge and information, but only a chosen few will do so with genuine care and from a loving spirit. Not everyone will be you.

ACKNOWLEDGEMENTS

I owe a great deal of appreciation to several individuals and organizations for their contributions, support and inspiration in bringing this project to fruition.

To Celeste Davis, thank you for your wonderful input and contributions to this text. You helped bring my vision to life and for that, I am forever grateful.

To my incredible editor Lisa Erby, thank you for not only taking on this project, but for doing so with the love, care, and enthusiasm as if it were your very own. This would not have been complete without you.

To my good friend Denard Williamson, thank you and your lovely wife Michelle, for your support and dedication to this work over the years. You have been a true blessing. TMP would not be what it is today without you.

To my fellow brothers of BMe Community, your unwavering commitment to our community and uplifting of Black Men in our society inspires me daily.

To my family, thank you for always lifting and encouraging me. No matter where we are- near or far, your continuous prayers and love reach me without fail. I love you all.

Lastly, to my boys. my young brothers. The young men of The Manhood Project. While I started this program in an effort to give, I am thankful for all that I have received. Seeing you all grow, learn and discover self has been more rewarding than I could have possibly imagined. Thank you for allowing me into your space and into your lives as you continue on your journeys. I love you all.

PRINCIPLES OF THE PROJECT
STRATEGIES FOR EFFECTIVE COACHING AND MENTORING

OUR STORY

(Coach Black and TMP students)

 "Manhood is about being present, not perfect." –Phil Black

"Genuine beginnings begin within us, even when they are brought to our attention by external opportunities."

-William Throsby Bridges

ABOUT US

The Manhood Project (TMP) is a coaching, mentoring and personal development program for boys ages 9 - 18. Our mission is to maximize the positive qualities of young men, while minimizing their temptations to engage in at-risk behaviors. The Manhood Project was founded in November of 2011. Starting as a pilot program, TMP began supporting a small group of 20 young men at Clark Preparatory Academy on Detroit's East Side. Today, TMP supports more than 150 young men throughout six schools and numerous community partnerships.

TMP was created as a testimony to the positive role models that I've encountered throughout my youth and the need to extend that same influence to young men in communities across the country. Using my life experiences as a platform, I've been able to use my emotional scars, as well as the help of family, friends, coaches, and mentors- as motivation to touch others and to help them grow and heal. Over time, I've built and maintained a reputation rooted in honesty, integrity, and professionalism- which has allowed me to assist multiple young men in correcting harmful behaviors. My approach to communication has been described as thought provoking, straight-forward and conversational- allowing for mentees and those I work with to converse at ease. I've continued to inspire and challenge communities to be more proactive and aid in improving the lives of those within their community. This guide is yet another step towards fulfilling that mission.

"Manhood is about being present, not perfect." –Phil Black

Since its inception, The Manhood Project has always believed and affirmed:

"Manhood is about being present, not perfect."

BEGINNINGS

The Manhood Project started as a response to an internal call to action within surrounding dilapidated communities. Over the years, I had personally become inundated with images, rhetoric, and statistics about the failing nature of black boys in America. Blame- that's all I could see and hear. People, everyday people that I interacted with and the larger societal representation, were pointing the finger solely at children for their shortcomings, poor academic performance, behavior, and societal outcomes. It was as if they had completely forgotten or chose to ignore the daily trauma, familial economic conditions, under-resourced communities, and even what we know about human development from a scientific perspective. Despite the conditions, mental, emotional, and physical restraints placed upon our boys from birth- none of that seemed to matter. "It's your own fault" seemed to be the popular notion, and that finger of judgement was not only pointed at our boys of today, I personally felt as if people were pointing directly at me.

Like many of these disadvantaged boys that people were shaming, my youth also included a tumultuous path that was very difficult to navigate. I was raised by a young, single mother in addition to the absence of my father within my life, left me with more questions than answers as I searched for guidance towards manhood. Countless memories of waiting plagued my memory. This nagging feeling of waiting for my father to arrive and to show up, has never left my memory. I wanted that guidance to come from him, but that

"Manhood is about being present, not perfect." –Phil Black

never happened. Fortunately for me, guidance came from those willing and able to be present.

My uncles taught me about family leadership, confidence, love, and support. They instilled in me what a healthy concept of manhood was, and I have always carried that with me. Even as I've faced hardships and overcome countless personal, professional, and spiritual hurdles, those learned concepts from my uncles have helped save me. After nearly taking my own life at the age of nine, as a result of deep depression and surviving a near fatal shooting as a college student, those conversations continued to guide and direct my path. In those dark moments their words and support of others (combined with my personal relationship with God) is what pulled me through. That was MY journey, but what about others that may be experiencing the same hardships and hurdles? "Someone needs to do something," I said to myself, while acknowledging my own experiences as a child within my mind.

The groundwork for TMP had finally been laid. After graduating from Highland Park High School in 1995, I frequented schools within the community, speaking and encouraging students at any given opportunity. In 2009, I volunteered as a local youth football coach and found the value in more direct one-on-one mentoring. As my professional career in Sales & Training began to flourish, I began formulating ideas about programs and what they could look like by engaging communities, as I traveled throughout the country. I spoke with close friends and colleagues about doing something significant. Now armed with

"Manhood is about being present, not perfect." –Phil Black

6

my personal experience, a professional background in sales, leadership, training, management, curriculum design, learning and development- the idea of a structured program just made sense. Ideas of this magnitude take just as much time to take shape, as they do to implement.

After taking a new role with City Year, LLC in 2010, I found myself more integrated into the local schools and youth development communities. I could see what worked and more importantly what failed as it related to young boys of color. I viewed our teachers being overwhelmed by the sheer weight of their roles. Often times, having to be counselor, mom, dad, friend, and psychologist- and that's just before the ringing of the first bell. Administrators were overworked and attempting to maintain some sort of balance, as they managed state, district, teacher, staff, student, and parental relationships. These same administrators also fought to meet student needs, while attempting to maximize very limited resources. I could finally see where schools and communities had gaps in providing programs that could be the critical bridge, linking them to the socioemotional support and development they so desperately needed. Now, I felt a *different* finger pointed at me. This time it wasn't in judgement, instead, it was one of chance and challenge to step up to the plate.

In 2012, I was ready to take action, so I visited the principal at Clark Preparatory Academy to discuss an early idea of The Manhood Project, while asking to work with a group of boys who needed extra attention and direction. After reaching a decision, the **only**

"Manhood is about being present, not perfect." –Phil Black

7

instruction upon my agreement to work at Clark, was that I had to show up. *Consistently.* That one statement would not only become the motto for The Manhood Project, it also served as our mission and key to maintaining and building long lasting relationships:

"You don't have be perfect, but you do have to be present."

In the beginning, The Manhood Project started as a call to action, and will remain as such. It was my rebuttal to those fingers being pointed at disadvantaged boys, and by mere association-pointed at my younger self. It was my answer to the call, by giving other young men a fighting chance by using the same basic principles that others had given to me. Those principles, the ones that steered me into a healthier pathway, becoming a more productive member of society and within my community- began the foundation for The Manhood Project. Simply put, I knew that my life experiences – both positive and negative, would one day serve a bigger purpose in helping others heal and change their life paths.

The call to action was to help young men see, develop, and realize their full potential. As for me personally, I wanted to stop the finger pointing, blame and willful ignorance on the part of those that ignored the root causes of the problems. It was my hope that this program would inspire and challenge individuals, communities, and our society as a whole- to be more proactive. Knowing that together, we could create a

"Manhood is about being present, not perfect." –Phil Black

8

social climate, where the extending of helping hands would overshadow pointing judgmental fingers.

At the end of the day, TMP aims to inspire **LOVE**.

TODAY

Today, The Manhood Project has served over 800 students, nine different schools, several districts, and communities since 2012- through direct programming and independent workshops. Over the years, we've consistently found that:

☐ When presented with the opportunity, students show a high level of interest in TMP. Both schools and students alike, report enthusiasm for participating in a program like The Manhood Project. As a result, we are able to build great relationships with students while supporting them in their overall development. Students feel incredibly supported by the program.

☐ When students consistently attend, they are highly likely to meet program goals. These goals include demonstrated improved behavior, academic gains, and expressed favorable or a highly favorable attitude towards graduation and seeking postsecondary opportunities.

"Manhood is about being present, not perfect." –Phil Black

COACHING AND MENTORING

"I've learned that people will forget what you said, people will forget what you did, but people will never forget how you made them feel."

-Maya Angelou

WHAT IS COACHING AND MENTORING?

For years, communities have viewed the positive impact that both formal and informal coaching and mentoring programs have had on youth development.

These programs aim to:

- ☐ Increase school attendance
- ☐ Reduce crime and behavior-related outcomes
- ☐ Improve grades and skills
- ☐ Prepare for college readiness
- ☐ Introduce career interests and options
- ☐ Foster extracurricular interests
- ☐ Develop leaders
- ☐ Create social integration

It is likely that coaching and mentoring practices have been around since the beginning of time, as these practices are built upon a foundation of relationships. At the core of these practices comes change, where *"specific knowledge and skills are transferred from one to the other- but with the intention of fostering independence."*[1] That's the essence of it. However, coaching and mentoring programs can be tailored according to the audience(s) and desired outcomes. In many school-based settings, these programs usually provide access to skills or relationships that students otherwise would not have access to- due to lack of resources within their schools and communities.

---

[1] Garvey, B., Stokes, P., & Megginson, D. (2009). Coaching and mentoring: Theory and practice. Los Angeles: SAGE.

"Manhood is about being present, not perfect." –Phil Black

13

While there are nuances when defining the terms: coaching and mentoring separately, their roles together are fluid. A very basic dictionary definition describes a mentor as: an experienced and trusted adviser. Similarly, a coach is defined as: an instructor or trainer. Furthermore, mentoring can be general practice while coaching can be grounded on a special set of skills and processes. Together, they provide a rich experience when focused on a set of desired outcomes through a programmatic structure.

Outcomes-based mentoring can be categorized into two types: instrumental (topic-focused) and psychosocial (open-ended). Instrumental mentoring is often focused on action and activities to address a specific problem or reach a specific goal. Psychosocial mentoring focuses on positive youth development and the process. Additionally, mentoring relationships are categorized as developmental or prescriptive. While prescriptive relationships are based on a mentor-defined set of goals and expectations, developmental relationships are more flexible based on the youth's needs and interests.[2] [3] In many modern day mentoring programs, you'll see a merging of these approaches and relationships-

---

[2] Jekielek, S., Moore K. A., & Hair, E. C. (2002). Mentoring programs and youth development: A synthesis. Washington, DC: Child Trends.

[3] Darling, N., Bogat, G. A., Cavell, T. A., Murphy, S. E., & Sánchez, B. (2006). Gender, ethnicity, development, and risk: Mentoring and the consideration of individual differences. Journal of Community Psychology J. Community Psychol., 34(6), 765-779.

"Manhood is about being present, not perfect." –Phil Black

taking into account all perspectives and needs of both mentor and mentee.

WHY MENTORING WORKS

Coaching and mentoring programs have proven themselves as an invaluable aspect of youth development. Mentoring can positively affect a young man's life by providing socioemotional support, scholastic, professional, or personal guidance in meeting predetermined goals. While mentoring in itself does not keep them away from negative influences, mentoring does provide an alternative perspective and support in the decision-making process. As a result, the mentee becomes more resourceful when faced with potential harmful situations and negative people.[4]

Noted in the landmark report The Mentoring Effect, there are many insights on the positive outcomes that mentoring provides. For instance:

- Young adults who face an opportunity gap, but have a mentor, are 55% more likely to be enrolled in college than those who did not have a mentor.
- Mentoring results in positive activities that translate into the higher self-esteem and self-confidence.
- Most youth report positive and helpful experiences with mentors.
- Mentees want to pay it forward and serve as mentors as well.

---

[4] Benefits for Young People. (n.d.). Retrieved September 08, 2016, from http://youth.gov/youth-topics/mentoring/benefits-mentoring-young-people

"Manhood is about being present, not perfect." –Phil Black

16

◻ Mentoring has a positive result on adult volunteers- encouraging them to be active and consistent volunteers within their own communities.[5]

In recent years, mentoring programs that target young people of disadvantaged backgrounds have become more prevalent in community outreach initiatives. With the creation of programs like: President Obama's My Brother's Keeper, there is a large push to eliminate the opportunity gap between men of color and non-Hispanic white men. The elimination of such opportunity gaps can lead to a higher quality of life, lower rates of incarceration, and healthier, better educated adults.[6]

GAPS IN MENTORING PROGRAMS

Approximately 16 million youth, including nine million at-risk youth, have never had a mentor of any kind. To put that into perspective, that means that only one in three young adults failed to receive mentoring of

---

[5] Bruce, Mary and Bridgeland, John (2014). *The Mentoring Effect: Young People's Perspectives on the Outcomes and Availability of Mentoring.* Washington, D.C.: Civic Enterprises with Hart Research Associates for MENTOR: The National Mentoring Partnership.
[6] Economic Costs of Youth Disadvantage and High-Return Opportunities for Change (Rep.). (2015, July). Retrieved September 8, 2016, from My Brothers Keeper website: https://www.whitehouse.gov/sites/default/files/docs/mbkreport_fi nal.pdf

"Manhood is about being present, not perfect." –Phil Black

any kind while growing up.[7] Understanding the benefits of mentorship and the potential behavior changes it provides, the need is clear. Informal and formal programs are high in demand, as are mentors, to even start addressing the needs and correct detrimental behaviors that at-risk youth are prone to.

Of the 66% of surveyed young people that reported having a mentor, over half only had an informal mentor (mentors not arranged through a program structure, but through other relationships). Some (11%) had both an informal and a formal mentor (mentor arranged through a structured program), while 4% only had a formal mentor. In other words, of the two-thirds of youth who reported having been mentored, fewer than 5% derived their mentoring solely from a mentoring program. What's more, informal mentoring lasted about 30 months on average, compared to roughly 18 months for its counterpart. So, combining frequency and duration, American kids received about eight times as much more informal versus formal mentoring. We can conclude that those who have informal mentors generally come from privileged or affluent backgrounds.

---

[7] Bruce, Mary and Bridgeland, John (2014). *The Mentoring Effect: Young People's Perspectives on the Outcomes and Availability of Mentoring.* Washington, D.C.: Civic Enterprises with Hart Research Associates for MENTOR: The National Mentoring Partnership.

"Manhood is about being present, not perfect." –Phil Black

FUTURE OF MENTORING

With qualitative and quantitative data supporting the benefits of mentoring, and a call to action for more mentoring programs, the opportunity for informal and formal mentoring programs is fertile. National resources and support, including technical assistance programs, support the growth of mentoring programs. Organizations offering mentoring as a part of college and career readiness through experiential learning are increasing. Other national organizations support local mentoring and youth development programs through chapters dispersed across the country, expanding their reach and hands-on approach. As schools struggle to find ways to supplement programming for students, independent and school-based mentoring programs will be necessary to ensure the success of students.

Using a holistic approach to integrate mentoring into schools and communities in order to drive achievement- will help close the current mentoring gap. The Mentoring Effect, the landmark report highlighting the impacts of mentoring programming, suggests the following:

- Program integration of mentoring with other national initiatives
- Expanding local, state, and federal public policy
- Using a standard mentoring structure to ensure quality of mentoring programs
- Increase support of private sector engagement

"Manhood is about being present, not perfect." –Phil Black

- Driving connections between research and practice
- Exploring innovative approaches[8]

Understanding a more inclusive landscape of resources and needs, will help expand mentoring programs and make them more accessible to all students. There is no one size fits all approach, however- a more cohesive and structured support system to expand the opportunities for program growth and success, is the most beneficial path to closing mentoring gaps.

---

[8] Bruce, Mary and Bridgeland, John (2014). *The Mentoring Effect: Young People's Perspectives on the Outcomes and Availability of Mentoring*. Washington, D.C.: Civic Enterprises with Hart Research Associates for MENTOR: The National Mentoring Partnership.

"Manhood is about being present, not perfect." –Phil Black

TMP MODEL - FOUNDATIONS

(TMP Alum, Codaro Shaw, receiving a hug from a current TMP student at Madison High School. 2016)

"Change will not come if we wait for some other person or some other time. We are the ones we've been waiting for. We are the change that we seek."

-President Barack Obama

"Manhood is about being present, not perfect." –Phil Black

FIVE VIRTUES

Personal virtues are characteristics valued as promoting collective and individual greatness. In addition to the standard learning and development tools that structure The Manhood Project, TMP also focuses on developing characteristics that embody the main focus of the program, which is manhood. Integrating personal experience and spirituality foundations, the Five Virtues are goals for the students to develop toward, as they approach their potential. In essence, the Five Virtues are necessary to be productive members of society through manhood.

LOVE
TMP's virtue of love is characterized as: learning to first love self- makes it possible to love others. As a virtue, love represents human kindness, compassion, and affection through *"the unselfish loyal and benevolent concern for the good of another."*[9] It may also describe compassionate and affectionate actions towards other humans and one's self.

RESPECT
TMP's virtue of respect teaches that: when you give respect, you are more likely to receive it. Respect is *"a feeling of admiring someone or something that is good, valuable, important- or a feeling/ understanding*

---

[9] "Love - Definition of love by Merriam-Webster". merriam-webster.com.

that someone or something is important, serious, etc., and should be treated in an appropriate way."[10]

COURAGE
TMP's virtue of courage is about having the strength to be yourself, no matter what you face or who is watching. Courage is defined as the ability to do something that you know is difficult or dangerous[11], and more specifically, moral courage is the ability to act rightly in the face of perceived popular opposition, shame, discouragement, or personal loss.

PROVISION
TMP's virtue of provision teaches every man must possess the ability and willingness to provide for himself and for his family. Provision is also defined as *"something that is done in advance to prepare for something else."*[12] Here, provision focuses on foresight and preparation based on one's vision.

PROTECTION
TMP's virtue of protection teaches that we must protect all that has been entrusted to us- especially those who cannot protect themselves. Additionally, protection is defined as a person or preventing someone or something from suffering harm or injury.

---

[10] "Respect - Definition of respect by Merriam-Webster". merriam-webster.com.
[11] "Courage - Definition of courage by Merriam-Webster". merriam-webster.com.
[12] "Provision - Definition of provision by Merriam-Webster". merriam-webster.com.

"Manhood is about being present, not perfect." –Phil Black

"Manhood is about being present, not perfect." –Phil Black

MODULES

Using a four-part modular approach to coaching and personal development, The Manhood Project uses these modular curriculum structures to introduce and reinforce concepts of leadership development- that aids in the personal growth of its participants. Modular learning arranges each part of the module, so that they complete one another. Each module provides knowledge and skills towards proficiency in a particular subject or learning outcome.

Modules help provide a framework for clear and realistic learning objectives. A module aims at developing a clearly identifiable and certifiable portion of the curriculum, expressed in terms of competence objectives. Therefore, modules aim high – to enable learners to achieve a level of development, which should be described in terms other than behavioral change or memorizing the Five Virtues.

Additionally, modular organization implies constant monitoring and feedback to ensure that learning is really a work-in-progress. One aspect, unique of TMP modules, is that they are interwoven throughout all units of the curriculum and not approached as separate objectives within the lessons and learnings. In this sense, the modules are cornerstones for which the curriculum structure stands.

"Manhood is about being present, not perfect." –Phil Black

The four modules of The Manhood Project curriculum are:

- **Exposure**
- **Education**
- **Engagement**
- **Encouragement**

EXPOSURE aims to provide students with real life examples of the lessons within The Manhood Project. Exposure is important because it allows students to gain insight to different paths and necessary self-potential. Essentially, TMP believes that one can only envision potential based on awareness and exposure. If one has not been exposed to potential, then it may not be realized. Exposure takes the lessons and applies them in a tangible way. As with most mentoring, exposure is important because it *"can offer advice, share life experiences, and help a young person navigate challenges."*[13]

Exposure takes place through powerful and impactful speakers and mentors that share their stories of struggle and triumph. Additionally, TMP identifies field trip opportunities to supplement classroom lessons. Other exposure methods within the curriculum include: reading, research, and visual resources.

EDUCATION directs the lessons with structured, educational workshops based on core areas of

---

[13] Mentoring Impact - MENTOR. (n.d.). Retrieved September 9, 2016, from http://www.mentoring.org/why-mentoring/mentoring-impact/

"Manhood is about being present, not perfect." –Phil Black

development and learning. The objective for education is to equip students with concrete knowledge that they are otherwise not exposed to during school or outside activities through an enlightening experience. Providing learning to the student also places a focus on equitable outcomes. With increased knowledge, students are able to be more productive, independent, and motivated. Collectively, all of this helps students remain competitive, driven, and attracted to increased opportunities they may come across. Each lesson focuses on a topic and incorporates a learning component within activities and discussion.

Community **ENGAGEMENT** places students within service-learning and civic engagement opportunities, as well as within activities that build character and overall growth. The curriculum also focuses all lessons on how students engage with school and everyday communities, which result in positive behavioral changes.

Putting thoughts into action is one of the reasons why engagement plays a major role within our modular learning system. Often, students are taught how to behave and what is expected of them, but engagement allows them a space to exhibit the learned behavior within a real-world setting. Engagement also expands how students interact with the world through volunteer and altruistic endeavors.

Through **ENCOURAGEMENT**, TMP acknowledges all steps of student progress, by positive affirmations from facilitators, fellow students, school, and everyday

"Manhood is about being present, not perfect." –Phil Black

community- allowing students to continue to make greater and sustainable gains. Encouragement is reflected both informally and formally throughout the lessons.

Encouragement reinforces positive behavior and is very forgiving, if there are missteps along the way. With encouragement, tools for change are not only reinforced, but also reiterated through words and through the peer examples. Encouragement does not punish or discipline; it simply motivates students to keep trying with the aid of positive support.

TMP MODEL - CURRICULUM

(TMP Brenda Scott Academy Students conducting a quiz review. 2016)

"Manhood is about being present, not perfect." –Phil Black

"One looks back with appreciation to the brilliant teachers, but with gratitude to those who touched our human feelings. The curriculum is not so much necessary raw material, but warmth is the vital element for the growing plant and for the soul of the child."

-Carl Jung

CURRICULUM OVERVIEW

Unit 1: Defining Manhood and Self Image
Lesson plans to:
- Establish norms, expectations and goal setting for program participation
- Help participants define a positive, healthy meaning for manhood
- Guide students through a reflection of behavior and self- image

Unit 2: Appropriate Communication
Lesson plans to:
- Differentiate between types of communication
- Help participants build tools for healthy communication
- Practice healthy communication methods

Unit 3: The Choice: Education or Prison?
Lesson plans to:
- Give background on School to Prison Pipeline
- Help participants understand current systems landscape
- Give students tools to advocate for themselves and their peers

Unit 4: The Importance of Showing Up (Presence Over Perfection)
Lesson plans to:
- Help participants establish behaviors of responsibility and commitment
- Cultivate acts of service to others in the community
- Exercise consistency and reliability in activities

"Manhood is about being present, not perfect." –Phil Black

Unit 5: Living the Five Virtues
Lesson plans to:
- ☐ Explore TMP Five Virtues of Manhood
- ☐ Understand the importance of the Five Virtues
- ☐ Learn how to implement the Five Virtues in daily life practice

Unit 6: Discipline, Self-Guidance, and Leadership
Lesson plans to:
- ☐ Give students tools to execute positive behavior change
- ☐ Provide methods for students to support and encourage others to exhibit positive behaviors
- ☐ Create long-lasting positive and impactful behavior

"Manhood is about being present, not perfect." –Phil Black

33

CURRICULUM FORMATION AND FOUNDATIONS

The Manhood Project's curriculum is also grounded on several models of youth learning, adult learning and development. These theories are woven within all of the lessons and sessions throughout the program. These theories provide TMP with proven tools to present information to participants while strengthening the outcomes of our mentorship program.

"Manhood is about being present, not perfect." –Phil Black

BACKGROUND

Upon discovering models of learning and development, it was clear that the foundation for The Manhood Project needed to be one that was exceptionally strong. Throughout my own professional and personal experiences, I've infused models that proved effective for me in many capacities. These models include: (but are not limited to) the Instructional Design Theory model, known as ADDIE, Maslow's Hierarchy, Hemispheric Integration, Acceptance Commitment Therapy or ACT Coaching, and the youth developmental theory and model-Clover.

In the year of 2006, I was introduced to the ADDIE Model by Marc Shogreen, a co-worker on the National Training Team for an indirect company of T-Mobile. I first met Marc after earning my 5th promotion within the company, which advanced me from the Detroit Market Trainer, to the National Sales Trainer. I was promoted mainly because of my ability to create trainings and teach others how to incorporate many of the strategies that made me a successful sales representative and manager. However, the trainings I created lacked structure, key elements needed to measure learning- all of which I found out quickly after Marc reviewed my material. As he deemed my designs as "utter garbage" he finished his critique by acknowledging my raw talent, and introducing me to the model of ADDIE. ADDIE helped me see how to develop my skills and give my trainings the structure and efficiency they needed.

"Manhood is about being present, not perfect." –Phil Black

ADDIE

The Instructional Systems Design Theory: ADDIE Model is the process traditionally used by instructional designers and training developers. The five phases: Analyze, Design, Develop, Implement, and Evaluate- represent a dynamic, flexible guideline for building effective training and performance support tools.

ANALYZE: This first step is the most important, as it is meant to help identify the actual needs of your audience and narrow the focus of your programming or training. Prior to creating TMP, I saw many needs in addition to developmental support (financial assistance, housing, tutoring, parent engagement, etc.). While I may have been able to make an impact in any one of those areas, my strengths were in Learning and Development- so that is what I chose to focus on.

DESIGN: Once you have made an exhaustive list of needs, narrow your focus by determining which needs you are best equipped to meet- then DESIGN the framework to suit those designated needs. This phase is also referred to as scaffolding. We'll convert raw needs into Learning Objectives, based on the type of knowledge that we wish to transfer to the learner (known as transferrable knowledge). There are three types of transferable knowledge: Know-Knowledge, Do-Knowledge, and Be-Knowledge.

1. Know-Knowledge is simply meant to increase a person's awareness around a particular topic. History is a good example of know-knowledge. While the information is beneficial in the sense

that it adds to the individual's perspective, there are no actionable expectations once learned.

2. Do-Knowledge is about skill building. When we recognize a negative gap between requirements and actual performance, it often points towards a deficiency in skills. Once identified, the learning focus becomes building the learner's capacity to complete (or do) a particular work by building that skill.

3. Be-Knowledge deals with a person's attitude. It is quite possible for someone to have both the knowledge and skills to perform, but have a poor attitude or lack motivation to execute their tasks. In this case, determining what barriers-either external or internal, may be preventing the individual from performing, will need to be addressed.

The Design step of ADDIE allows you to determine exactly what the learning outcomes should and will be. This is vital in measuring learning.

DEVELOP: Now that you have a strategic focus, evidenced by your objectives, developing the methods and materials, while listing resources that will help you meet the objectives, is next. This is where the decision was made to have group sessions and create lists for everything needed to make the sessions work. I also recognized the need for field trips, guest speakers, and additional framework.

"Manhood is about being present, not perfect." –Phil Black

IMPLEMENT: The rubber meets the road in this step. Now that the planning is complete, it is time to put it to work and begin testing. I decided to use one group for beta testing, although multiple groups are possible. The key is to start, implement the plan and see what works, without worrying about the outcome- as you are using pure information to gain future desired outcomes.

EVALUATE: Once you have implemented your learning plan, it is now time to evaluate its effectiveness. Simply put, did you meet the learning objectives? Evaluation answers that question.

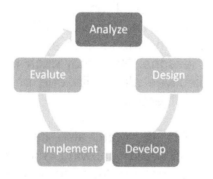

Notice that the illustration above, depicting the ADDIE model, is somewhat circular in shape. The reasoning behind that: creating any form of learning tool is an ongoing process. After evaluating whether your objectives have been met, you are now in a position to- if successful the first time, to test the material on another group. Or, if adjustments are needed- to make changes (either re-determining the needs, adjusting your learning objectives, introducing new tools or refining the implementation strategy) for the desired outcome.

For TMP, ADDIE largely represents things unseen within the general lessons or the programs focus. I've identified the needs of young men, but was forced to determine which of those needs I (and past trainees) could actually meet. Remember, when it comes to working with underserved or disadvantaged youth, the needs are vast- including financial support, transportation, clothing, shelter, academic tutoring, etc. No one individual or organization can effectively fill every single gap. ADDIE helps narrow the focus, to create programming that meets individual critical needs. One final note, I used ADDIE to not only create the focus and structure of TMP as a program and organization- the model was also used to create the individual lessons. Note that each unit and their respective objectives align with one or more of the overall program objectives.

In addition to ADDIE, Marc also introduced me to Maslow's Theory, and showing me how it was applicable in the space of learning and development. Through my personal research and practice of the theory- I quickly realized its effectiveness. After three years of building TMP, I also recognized a need to acquire more specialization and training. Particularly in the area of one on one engagement with youth and adults. Up until that very point, I had realized that most of my skills mainly focused on small group interactions. In January of 2015, I found a Life Coaching Certification program with the Spencer Institute based out of California.

"Manhood is about being present, not perfect." –Phil Black

MASLOW'S HIERARCHY OF NEEDS

Abraham Maslow created a model of human needs as a hierarchy to self-actualization, also known as Maslow's Hierarchy of Needs.[14] According to Maslow, basic needs are said to motivate people when they are unmet. One must satisfy lower level basic needs (like physiological needs of food, rest, warmth, and water) before progressing on to meet higher level growth needs. Maslow subsequently extended the idea to 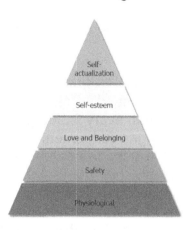 include his observations of humans' innate curiosity. His theories parallel many other theories of human developmental psychology, some of which focus on describing the stages of growth in humans.

TMP applies Maslow's Hierarchy primarily through the recognition of the stages daily- in both facilitation and specific rituals within the program.

PHYSIOLOGICAL: TMP not only provides basic snacks for students, TMP also makes snaking available at every session. During major events, the program also has full meals available to help encourage fellowship and aide with nourishment.

---

[14] Maslow, A. H. (1943). A Theory of Human Motivation. *Psychological Review*, 50(4), 370-96.

"Manhood is about being present, not perfect." –Phil Black

Satisfying this basic need, not only minimizes distractions- but it also helps build rapport. When a student is willingly fed, without any expectations in return, he begins to view the program in a different light, and the facilitator as someone who genuinely cares- which works to breakdown many of the walls that exist.

SAFETY: TMP's first norm is SAFE SPACE- based on a basic need of safety. The program attempts to ensure that every student feels safe and protected from: danger, judgement, or otherwise. Another TMP norm that supports safety is the Man Law of: "never sharing another man's business." Meaning, what is said in confidence amongst TMP members, should remain in that room (as long as no one presents a danger to others or themselves).

LOVE/BELONGING: This sense of love/belonging is also reflected in our norms and general approach to programming- particularly Safe Space, Respect and NOSTUESO (No One Speaks Twice Until Everyone Speaks Once). Additionally, our frequent group activities and dialogs support this need- for connectedness.

ESTEEM: Part of TMP's goal is to build the confidence of young men as well as their ability to express themselves. TMP uses a strategy of encouragement that is "on time, relevant and often." In itself, our motto seeks to promote a conscious and continuous attitude towards always putting forth your best effort.

"Manhood is about being present, not perfect." –Phil Black

SELF-ACTUALIZATION: Typically around the middle and towards the end of the program, TMP begins to see many of the participants displaying recognizable change. For some, it is seen in their appearance and for others- it is present in their attitude, demeanor, behavior, and overall performance. Maslow's Theory has proven to be an incredible tool, ensuring the elements of TMP programming have a measurable purpose.

The online program also gave me an insight into the world of individual coaching and offered various science-based strategies that helped me differentiate between mentoring and coaching. Yet, the most valuable take-away, and what presents itself most often in TMP, is the knowledge I've gained regarding brain development. That knowledge was derived from studying the cornerstone strategy called Hemispheric Integration- a process by which individuals access information from both sides of the brain (right/emotional and left/logical) to become fully resourceful when making decisions and taking action.

HEMISPHERIC INTEGRATION

My first Certification Program as a Life coach centered around the science based practice of Hemispheric Integration. While our life experiences are typically cataloged and described as singular events, scientifically- we experience them on multiple levels, two being: emotionally (or through our right brain) and logically (or through our left brain). As is the case with other senses, such as sight, one side tends to dominate over the other and becomes the primary lens by which we view, receive, process, and respond to information.

Example:
While walking down the hall, John accidentally bumps into Chris. If he is right brain dominant and has not developed the proper skills to see the events logically, Chris might get upset, yell or even hit John.

Hemispheric Integration therapy provides tools to help individuals access both sides of their brain- in an effort to become more resourceful when responding to situations. By using Hemispheric Integration therapy, one will take information from both sides (acknowledging the emotion, while seeing the linear progression) to determine the best response to any given situation. While we have integrated some of the strategies into the TMP curriculum, particularly when working one on one and within the My Journey section, the information regarding brain development has been most beneficial.

Through my studies, I've learned that on a fundamental level, the human brain does not fully develop at the earliest, until the mid-twenties in age. Some studies even suggested full development happening in our early 30's.[15] [16] For me this was a

---

[15] Edwards, L. (2010, December 22). Retrieved September 11, 2016, from http://m.phys.org/news/2010-12-brain-fully-mature-30s-40s.html

[16] Holloway, B., & Roux, S. (n.d.). Understanding the Teen Brain. Retrieved September 11, 2016, from

game changer. An unexpected eye opener in that I was now able to better understand how and why, many of our young men (and youth in general) could possibly make some of the unhealthy decisions that they do.

The right side (the emotional side) of our brain is fully developed at birth. Consider this: babies are born with the innate ability to cry, smile, or become angry- this statement makes total sense as those displays of emotion are natural occurrences. On the other hand, the left brain (the logical side), which governs our reasoning and controls the frontal lobe, is mostly responsible for processing information and critical thinking. Unlike emotions, our thought processes continue to develop as we grow and learn. This fundamental truth helped shape how I viewed our young men and women in a completely different light. This knowledge alone, has helped me to be more patient, gave me greater awareness in focusing on their development- rather than being quick to judge. In short, I've gained a whole new level of understanding to the common phrase "he has some growing to do."

Later that year, I was introduced to ACT Coaching by Dr. Leah Mazzola, the founder of the Youth Coaching Institute located in Dallas, Texas. I studied under Dr. Mazzola for 30 weeks to earn my second certification as a Life and Youth Coach. ACT has helped me to recognize the power that lies in simply helping others to see their own strengths and abilities, so that they'll

---

https://www.urmc.rochester.edu/encyclopedia/content.aspx?ContentTypeID=1

"Manhood is about being present, not perfect." –Phil Black

44

become unstuck in their ways, and begin achieving their goals. Contrary to popular life coaching methods, ACT is not a system built around positive affirmations, pep talks, or tough love exercises. ACT is about helping a person achieve daily balance, by aligning their actions with their personal values.

ACT COACHING

Acceptance and Commitment Therapy (ACT)- is a form of psychotherapy commonly described as a combination of Cognitive-Behavioral Therapy (CBT) or Clinical Behavioral Analysis (CBA).[17] It is an empirically-based psychological intervention, that uses a multifaceted combination of strategies (acceptance, mindfulness, commitment, and behavior-change) to increase psychological flexibility.[18]

Principles of ACT, are integrated into the TMP curriculum in many different ways. Most prominently, when communicating with students about particular goals, ACT strategies are applied to help guide their thinking- instead of thinking for them.

Like Hemispheric Integration, ACT is present in both the One on Ones and My Journey sections and the

---

[17] Plumb, J., Stewart, I., Dahl, G., & Lundgren, T. (2009, Spring). In Search of Meaning: Values in Modern Clinical Behavior Analysis. Behav Anal, 31(1), 85-103.

[18] Hayes, S. (n.d.). ACT | Association for Contextual Behavioral Science. Retrieved September 9, 2016, from https://contextualscience.org/act

"Manhood is about being present, not perfect." –Phil Black

information is all mentee-focused. Rather than giving advice, the facilitator is simply guiding thought. The main reason for this lies in the difference between mentoring and coaching. As a mentor, the mentor is the expert. A mentor has all the knowledge and, in most cases, is simply giving that knowledge to the mentee. As a coach, the student is the expert of himself - his life and his experiences. While TMP takes the approach of both, leading towards the coaching role, by working to teach students how to make decisions for themselves based upon their personal goals and values.

Lastly, my exposure to the Clover model took place while working with City Year, LLC in 2011. While participating in a leadership development opportunity, offered by the PEAR Institute of Boston, a select number of managers- myself included, were introduced to the model. The Clover model provides a common language and structure for working with and developing youth.

CLOVER
Clover is a socioemotional development model and tool- used to promote positive learning and development in youth and adults. Clover was created by Dr. Gil Noam of The PEAR Institute in collaboration with Harvard Medical School and the McLean Hospital.

Building on the work of many past youth development theorists, Dr. Noam identified the four key ingredients that all people need- to thrive and learn:

"Manhood is about being present, not perfect." –Phil Black

- Active Engagement
- Assertiveness
- Belonging
- Reflection

In his studies, Dr. Noam realized that, similar to traditional stage model theory, humans tend to specialize in one of these four ingredients (or Clover Leaves as they are depicted in the model) at different times during our developmental ages (0-5 Active Engagement, 6-10 Assertiveness, 11-14 Belonging and 15+ Reflection). However, unlike traditional stage model theory, Clover recognizes that while there are indeed "key times for specialization" all four leaves are present and developing at all times. For example, a child at the "terrible twos" age is still experiencing and learning the world through touch and other senses (Active Engagement). Yet, we also see them beginning to show "Assertiveness" (which is about our desire to make our own decisions) by using words like "No." Learning Clover helped me to understand the students that I worked with, by having the ability to recognize: the "Leaf they are living in," viewing the strengths of that leaf- to be aware of its challenges and to identify ways to support growth and balance.[19]

TMP applies Clover in the designing of TMP lessons, activities, classroom set up, and facilitation strategies.

---

[19] PEAR – Partnerships in Education, And Resilience. Retrieved September 08, 2016, from http://www.pearweb.org/about/Clover.html

Clover is represented in the many strategies present in most, if not, all lessons within the curriculum. I have placed some type of physical movement in most of the lessons. TMP gives space for "voice and choice" or assertiveness through cultivating healthy discussions. Activities are pair or group-based to support "belonging" (which is about discovering one's self through relationships with others). Finally, students receive ample opportunities to reflect, through many of our writing exercises and times-explicitly reserved for reflection.

"Manhood is about being present, not perfect." –Phil Black

LESSON PLAN ELEMENTS

The Manhood Project incorporates specific elements into each session in order to create a safe and positive space for students. Creating a safe and positive space, allows students to learn and absorb the information presented. Each lesson element serves a purpose in both format and placement within the lesson. All elements work cohesively, to give students an agenda, and to be prepared for every session. This also helps the students actively participate and be leaders within their classroom. Understanding what to expect and consistency- are key underlying behavioral expectations of both TMP participants and facilitators. A regular flow of activity in the lesson will bring order, direction, and structure to each session.

SNACK AND CHAT:

The impetus for Snack and Chat is to simply meet a basic human need of food before the session begins. It is important to allow time for students to engage freely with one another once they come together. Snack and Chat is the specific time allotted for them to simply unwind from the day, share stories or simply engage in general conversation. TMP has made sure that time is uninterrupted by the facilitator. This time is imperative to refuel on energy, meet basic needs, and prepare for full attention during the lesson. Snacks generally include a combination of juice or water, and two to three of the following: (depending on the time of the session [morning, early or late afternoon]) breakfast bar, fruit cup, fruit snacks, baked chips, fruit,

"Manhood is about being present, not perfect." –Phil Black

pudding, applesauce, etc. While students will not likely fill-up on any of these, we have found that two - three snacks, plus a drink ratio- is enough to take the edge off, improve focus- and when done consistently over time, does wonders towards fostering a great relationship rooted in genuine care.

HIGHLIGHTS OR DO-OVERS:

Highlights or Do-Overs (H&Ds) are the part of the lesson where the facilitator gets to engage students about their weekend, previous day, etc. Each willing participant shares one highlight and/or a "do-over" since their last session. A highlight is a positive activity or experience that the participant had. On the other hand, a "do-over" would be an adverse situation that recently occurred within the student's life- that they wish they could do all over again. In this sense, the adverse situation is a challenge, and if given the opportunity to rewind time, the student would handle the situation differently to experience a better outcome (e.g. an argument, low grade on a test, etc.).

Sessions that celebrate both success and challenges, build the comfort necessary for participants to: ask critical questions, share ideas, participate in honest and open discussions. Starting with celebrations and lessons learned, are a short and easy way to create a safe space for students and encourage them to take risks. This specific group interaction occurs, as a result of the fundamental concepts learned through formal ACT Coaching and Training. One example is applying Focused and *Global Listening* while students are sharing.

"Manhood is about being present, not perfect." –Phil Black

ACT teaches three levels of listening: internal, focused, and global. Internal listening, or level one, is characterized by self-talk, while the other person is speaking. Rather than hearing and processing their words, we begin to think about how what they are saying relates to or impacts us. To gauge if you are a level one listener, simply access your response. More often than not, when we are engaged in level one-internal listening, we respond with statements that are about ourselves but appear to relate to the other person's topic. "That reminds me of" or "I usually..." are example introductions to statements birthed from internal listening. Of course, we should do this intentionally when relating and building rapport with others. However, too many level one responses often create a disconnect between you and the other party- as they may begin to feel that the conversation is all about you. In most instances, while coaching, but during H&D's in particular, you want to use more focused and global listening.

Focused, or level two listening, is characterized by the undivided attention and complete "focus" placed on the other person and what they are saying. It is almost as if nothing else exists- except you and the other person you are speaking with. Imagine a basketball player standing at the free throw line, or a golfer lining up a putt- that is the essence of level two- clearing focused listening. Level three, or global listening, is characterized by the ability to hear what is unsaid. You become so connected with the other person, that you are able hear their words- while sensing deeper, relative information under the surface.

"Manhood is about being present, not perfect." –Phil Black

Learning and applying these skills and being connected to your students, aids the facilitator by: (1) remaining engaged with students in a genuine manner, (2) gaining more insight around their thoughts and deeper feelings and (3) ensure that the facilitator gives relevant and coherent responses that are completely focused on the students and their needs- while minimizing any temptation to give judging or self-serving responses.

REVIEW AND WARM UP:

The review is a brief recap of learned material from the previous session, to ensure that students are ready to move forward with new learning. Additionally, the warm up is an activity or discussion question that helps to prepare students for the lesson of the day. These activities are usually brief and allow students to fully engage in reviewing prior lessons and preparing for new material. While the review may be straightforward in approach, the warm up sometimes incorporates a creative approach to presenting the subject matter of the new material.

If a lesson fails to start off strong- by activating prior knowledge, creating anticipation, or establishing goals, the interest of the participant begins to wane, and the facilitator may have to do some heavy lifting to retrieve the participants back. Equally, if not more important- being mindful of students' individual and collective learning needs, is critical. Like all activities used in TMP, the curriculum specifically indicates that review and warm-up sections are catered to student needs, and should remain active, autonomous,

"Manhood is about being present, not perfect." –Phil Black

collaborative, and reflective. In short, the application of the Clover method is heavily used in the review and warm up sections.

LESSON:
This is the point in the session where the new material is presented to the participants. The lesson incorporates different learning methods such as introduction and presentation. While most of the theories that we've introduced (like Maslow, ACT, and Clover) will continuously be at work, we have found that remaining cognizant of presentation is important. Meaning, facilitators must present the lesson in such a way, that it speaks to each student's Visual, Auditory, Reading, and Kinesthetic (or VARK) learning style (which we will cover momentarily within this document.)

RECAP AND REFLECTION:
The recap part of the lesson is the review of the newly learned material from that day. Through reflection, the facilitator asks a probing question to help students further integrate the new material into their everyday perspective and outlook. If a lesson fails to check for understanding, the facilitator will never know if the goal of the lesson was attained. The reflection also prepares students for the following sessions that will build on, and compliment the newly learned information. In doing so, this builds the student's need for Reflection as suggested by the Clover model. Additionally- adult and adolescent learners have a need to connect new information to past, current or

"Manhood is about being present, not perfect." –Phil Black

future experiences, helping them to process and make relevant meaning of the new information.

CLOSE:

TMP ends each lesson with the closing pledge before the facilitator and participants part their ways. The pledge should be memorized by both- participants and facilitator- as soon as possible, as its recital is an important part of closing each lesson. When done consistently, and with passion- this short ritual goes a long way towards build team and creating a true sense of belonging. In all such instances, the group locks arms and makes a circle- while reciting the pledge to further exhibit connectedness among the group. You will know that you have given the proper attention to this critical element when students begin to compete over who gets to lead.

"Manhood is about being present, not perfect." –Phil Black

THE MANHOOD PROJECT PLEDGE

Leader: As we go...
Group: Keep us safe!

Leader: While we're apart...
Group: Keep us united!

Leader: So when we return...
Group: We will be even better!

Leader: For we are...
Group: SMART!

Leader: We are...
Group: STRONG!

Leader: We are...
Group: MEN!

Leader: Manhood on three... 1, 2, 3...
Group: MANHOOD!

"Manhood is about being present, not perfect." –Phil Black

LEARNING STYLES

The Manhood Project uses different learning styles to present and reinforce the lessons within the curriculum. The term "learning styles" speaks to the understanding that every student learns differently. Technically, a participant's learning style refers to the preferential way in which the participant absorbs processes, comprehends, and retains information. Neil Fleming's **VARK** model of Student Learning refers to the four types of learning styles: Visual, Auditory, Reading/Writing Preference, and Kinesthetic.

◻ Visual learners prefer the use of images, maps, and graphic organizers to access and understand new information.

◻ Auditory learners best understand new content through listening and speaking in situations such as lectures and group discussions. Aural learners use repetition as a student technique and benefit from the use of mnemonic devices.

◻ Students with a strong reading/writing preference learn best through words. These students may present themselves as copious note takers or avid readers, and are able to translate abstract concepts into words and essays.

◻ Students who are kinesthetic learners best understand information through tactile representations of information. These students are hands-on learners and learn best through figuring things out by hand.

Overall, the **VARK** model believes:

- Students' preferred learning modes have significant influence on their behavior and learning.

- Students' preferred learning modes should be matched with appropriate learning strategies.

- Information that is accessed through students' use of their modality preferences shows an increase in their levels of comprehension, motivation, and metacognition.[20]

ELEMENTS OF A MULTISENSORY LESSON

TMP lessons are written and delivered to connect to the learner's senses- or emotions, through themed units of study that allow the learner to connect to the material in a more visceral fashion. Multisensory makes use of all senses. Although they may not be used all at once, in most multisensory lessons, participants engage with the material in more than one way. If a participant learns something using more than one sense, the information is more likely to be

---

[20] Fleming, N., & Baume, D. (2006, November). Learning Styles Again: VARKing up the right tree! *Educational Developments, SEDA Ltd*, (7.4), 4-7.

retained. Multisensory learning can be particularly helpful for participants with learning, attention, and behavior challenges. Using multiple senses gives these (and other) participants more ways to connect with what they're learning. This type of hands-on learning can make it easier for students to:

- Collect information
- Make connections between new and established information
- Understand and work through problems
- Use nonverbal problem-solving skills

Multisensory instruction helps participants tap into their learning strengths, to not only make connections -but to also form memories. Additionally, it allows the students to use a wider range of tools to display what they've learned-[21] both of which are important to the TMP sessions.

SETTING UP THE CLASSROOM ENVIRONMENT FOR ALL LEARNING STYLES

Environmental stimuli has a significant impact on the learner. Classroom setup can dramatically affect the participants' attitudes toward learning and their habits of learning. Participants need an environment that is

---

[21] Morin, A. (2015). Multisensory Instruction: What You Need to Know. Retrieved September 09, 2016, from https://www.understood.org/en/school-learning/partnering-with-childs-school/instructional-strategies/multisensory-instruction-what-you-need-to-know

"Manhood is about being present, not perfect." –Phil Black

organized, stimulating, and comfortable- in order to learn effectively. Creating such an environment entails arranging a practical physical layout, supplying diverse materials, supplies, and encouraging students to have a sense of belonging and ownership. TMP sessions encourage a classroom set up for the group to be engaged during all activities. Desk arrangements that facilitate open communication and eye contact between participants and the facilitator are very important. Unnecessary stimuli and objects within the classroom should be put away as to not disturb the learning process.

LESSON PLANS AND ACTIVITIES
UNIT 1: DEFINING MANHOOD AND SELF IMAGE

We begin the program with this unit to set the foundation for the facilitator and participants- to establish intentions for one another. The facilitators are introducing the participants to the program and introducing them to the concept of manhood, under The Manhood Project framework. As participants, the students are reflecting on their own self- image, how it may relate to manhood, and introducing themselves to you and the other participants.

The purpose of the level setting is to get everyone- the facilitators and students, on the same page. This also sets the tone for expectations- not only in this unit, but in the units to come.

First, the lessons set the tone by setting expectations of how everyone will interact with one another as well as what they should derive from the program. Next, the lessons start to look inward and delve into self-reflecting- while building self-awareness.

Overall, these lesson plans are designed to:

◻ Establish norms, expectations, and goal setting for program participation
◻ Help participants define a positive and healthy meaning for manhood
◻ Guide students through a reflection of behavior and self-image

"Manhood is about being present, not perfect." –Phil Black

Here's a list of the topics included within the unit:

☐ Establishing Norms, Expectations, and Goal Setting
☐ Building a Positive and Inclusive Environment
☐ Defining Manhood
☐ At Risk Behavior
☐ Me and My Image

Establishing Norms, Expectations, and Goal Setting

☐ Determine acceptable and unacceptable conduct within the designated TMP space.
☐ Recognize the operational and communicative group norms.
☐ Identify what is expected of them (conduct, behavior changes, etc.) as a result of participating in the program.

THE MANHOOD PROJECT'S pre-determined norms:

SAFE SPACE: The TMP group session is an inclusive, sacred space that is free of judgment.

MAN LAW: Never share another man's business. When we come together, sensitive, and personal information is often shared. To maintain our safe space, we never share an individual's business.

RESPECT: We respect everyone's personal rights, experiences, and opinions.

NOSTUESO: No One Speaks Twice Until Everyone Speaks Once

SELF-CORRECT: Always work to correct your own behavior before anyone else does.

SLANT: Sit-up, Listen, Ask Questions, Nod your head yes or no (showing through body language your attentiveness) and Track the speaker.

BE PRESENT: Actively participate.

PHONES UP AND ON SILENT: Phones may only be used in emergencies. In an actual emergency, excuse yourself from the room. *This should not happen often for any one individual.

HANDS-UP, VOICES-UP: When working to get everyone back focused, the coach may use one of these strategies.

"Manhood is about being present, not perfect." –Phil Black

LEAVE IT BETTER THAN YOU FOUND IT: Make sure the meeting space is clean at the end of each session.

"Manhood is about being present, not perfect." –Phil Black

Throughout this lesson, the boys will complete activities and exercises, to establish unacceptable and acceptable behavior for themselves and the group. Establishing norms at the beginning of any group setting is very important. Norms are: "an agreement among members of a classroom or school, regarding how they'll treat one another."[22] The Manhood Project uses a combination of norms: safety, health, moral, and discretionary- to create an ideal learning space for the students. Norms present a healthy space for all students to learn information, engage with one another in a healthy way, and achieve their goals.

- Participants will communicate short (e.g. end of Unit I) and long term (e.g. end of the program) goals for themselves.

Goal setting for students allows them to establish where they want to go and how they want to get there. When students are aware of their own goals, they become cognizant of what they need to work on, and what they want to accomplish. This helps them focus, as well as self-motivate and assess their productivity throughout the program. Goal setting also allows students to articulate the goals that they'd like to accomplish and agree to. This ultimately helps with the building up of self-confidence- leading to other positive behavioral development as well.

---

[22] Finley, T. (2014). The Science Behind Classroom Norming. Retrieved September 08, 2016, from http://www.edutopia.org/blog/establishing-classroom-norms-todd-finley

<u>Building a Positive and Inclusive Environment</u>

- Appropriately introduce themselves to various individuals.
- Share facts about at least one person in the group.
- Express how learning about others, significantly affects their own sense of belonging.

Settings with more collaborative and "connected" modes of learning could be better suited for students of diverse backgrounds. These settings acknowledge personal experiences, examine the relationships between persons and ideas, while encouraging students to work together to produce knowledge while learning.[23] Creating a classroom tone that is friendly, caring and supportive, while allowing students to explore the relationship between course material, personal and social experiences- tends to enhance, rather than undermine, student learning. Adult Learning Theory assumes that: as a person matures- he/she accumulates a growing reservoir of experience that becomes an increasing resource for learning that is applicable to adolescent learners as well.[24]

---

[23] Brookes, A., Belenky, M. F., Clinchy, B. M., Goldberger, N. R., & Tarule, J. M. (1988). Women's Ways of Knowing: The Development of Self, Voice, and Mind. *Curriculum Inquiry*, 18(1), 113.

[24] Tough, A., & Knowles, M. S. (1985). Andragogy in Action: Applying Modern Principles of Adult Learning. *The Journal of Higher Education*, 56(6), 707.

MAN HOOD
THE
Project

"Manhood is about being present, not perfect." –Phil Black

In this lesson, students will work toward learning more about one another in order to facilitate a positive and inclusive learning environment. The activities within this lesson allow for an open flow of communication while building additional communication skills to share and gather information about their peers.

☐ Students will demonstrate and explain the TMP norms and communication tools.

Defining Manhood

☐ Identify a negative and a positive example of manhood.
☐ List the qualities that create a negative image of manhood.
☐ Define a poor example of manhood.
☐ Express ways to avoid becoming the negative example.

This session establishes and presents TMP's framework of manhood to the students. Frameworks provide guidance to the standards of an ideal- that must be adhered to under the programs purview. In other words, curriculum frameworks are organized plans or set learning outcomes that define the content to be learned in terms of clear, definable standards, of what the student should know and be able to do. The framework is the first step in defining clear, attainable and high standards- that will be achieved by all students.

"Manhood is about being present, not perfect." –Phil Black

During the review of this lesson, the students reiterate the fundamental information and group norms. This fundamental information, which provides the framework of manhood for TMP, includes the Five Virtues of Manhood, the Creed of Men, which includes the organization's motto.

CREED OF MEN

We love according to the commandment.
We know respect must start from within, given and
earned, before it can be received.
We are courageous enough to be ourselves and not
follow the negative influences of others.
We vow to provide for our households while helping
others in need.
We protect all that is entrusted to our care and those
who cannot defend themselves.
In times of fear and doubt, we remind ourselves and
each other:
"You don't have to be perfect, but you must be
present."

For these are the measures of a man

"Manhood is about being present, not perfect." –Phil Black

At Risk Behavior

- ☐ Express what it means to be at-risk.
- ☐ List examples of at-risk behaviors (ARB's).
- ☐ Communicate what ARB's they have personally engaged in prior to joining the program.
- ☐ Explain possible short and long term consequences to exemplifying ARB's.

My Image and I

- ☐ List the personal behaviors that they would like to change.
- ☐ Acknowledge how others view them.
- ☐ Explain the difference between a person's self-image and reputation.
- ☐ Identify ways to build a good reputation and maintain a positive self-image.
- ☐ Recognize how the perception of others can affect our reputation.
- ☐ Explain the difference between a person's self-image and their reputation.
- ☐ Determine which factors help to build one's self-image and reputation.
- ☐ Acknowledge how others view them.

Low achievement and behavior challenges are often a result of a negative self-image or low self-esteem. Additionally, as developmental changes are constantly in motion for adolescents- identity formation is often hard to understand. Identity can come in the forms of how we perceive ourselves, how others perceive us, and how we interpret others seeing us.

Excerpt from *Identity: A Path to Self-Esteem* by Gwendolyn Hampton

Self-acceptance is a springboard for all our successes and failures. It is a particularly difficult task for the adolescent. The familiar and comfortable self we knew in childhood is in a state of change. All the changes in his body (i.e. sexual development, physical size, and muscular development) and changes in his cognitive development necessitate a modification of his childhood self.

He is constantly told by others that he is growing up, and with this growth comes new responsibilities, certain rights and advantages, and expected behaviors. Added to the changes and expectations is the conflict that arises between the internalization of values accepted by society and the need to reject those values in favor of what his conscience tells him is right or wrong. Consequently, he begins to ask questions such as: "Who am I?" "What do I believe in?" "Would others like me if they knew what kind of person I am?"

These changes and new attitudes of mind are a source of anxiety for the adolescent, partly because he does not have a clearly defined sense of self and cannot instantaneously become an adult, and he has to learn to accept his particular person. Until he can get through these obstacles, he is apt to have low self-esteem."[25]

[25] Hampton, G. (1984). Identity: A Path to Self-Esteem. American Adolescents in the Public Eye, 5. Retrieved September

"Manhood is about being present, not perfect." –Phil Black

UNIT 2: APPROPRIATE COMMUNICATION

Unit 2 focuses on communication. The purpose of this unit is to establish that the way people use communication extends beyond the words used to express thoughts and feelings. Communication can include body language, the vehicles used to communicate, and who communicates with whom. Often, physical behavior is not considered during communication; as it's innate. This unit will allow the participants to study, reflect, and improve their communication skills- to foster better relationships and outcomes.

Understanding how to communicate in a healthy way is an essential building block. TMP address communication early within the curriculum because it is often the key to unlocking a multitude of healthy behaviors while addressing past unhealthy behaviors. Our study of communication addresses expression in multiple forms.

Overall, these lesson plans are designed to:

□   Differentiate between types of communication
□   Help participants build tools for healthy communication
□   Practice healthy communication methods

8, 2016, from
http://teachersinstitute.yale.edu/curriculum/units/1984/5/84.05.06.x.html

"Manhood is about being present, not perfect." –Phil Black

Here's a list of the topics discussed within the unit:

- Communication 101 - Defining Communication
- Communication 102 - Environments and Individuals
- Communication and Technology
- Understanding Communicative Spaces
- Reputation Impact

<u>Communication 101 - Defining Communication</u>

- Define Communication
- List examples of the two main types of communication (verbal and nonverbal)
- Explain what is meant by the phrase: "you are always communicating."
- Express the importance of being aware of your communication

Addressing communication early in the curriculum is important as it is the basis for all self-expression and relationship building. Through communication, participants learn to build rapport, trust, and respect. Communication skills include: reading, writing, listening, and speaking. "Expressing thoughts clearly, crisply articulating opinions, communicating coherent instructions, motivating others through powerful speech - these skills have always been valued in the workplace and in public life."[26] Communication skills

---

[26] *The Intellectual and Policy Foundations of the 21st Century Skills Framework* (Rep.). (2007). Retrieved September 8, 2016,

"Manhood is about being present, not perfect." –Phil Black

also include nonverbal communication. Nonverbal communication includes everything from facial expressions to body language.

The facilitator has an important role within this session. The facilitator must be a teacher, mentor, as well as a role model. Communication skills must be taken very seriously, as they cannot be mastered until becoming first nature. Participants must not only see what effective communication looks and feels like; they must also understand the details of how and why it should be executed properly, so that they can practice and hone their skills.

Communication 102 - Environments and Individuals

- Discuss what it feels like to be in an unfamiliar environment.
- Identify specific behaviors or elements which make them uncomfortable in new spaces.
- Share methods used to overcome any insecurities or anxieties felt when adapting to an environment or person.
- Communicate the importance of being aware of the spaces we occupy.

Many of our communication methods - verbal and nonverbal expression - are the result of a situation and how we perceived it at that moment in time. Here,

from Partnership for 21st Century Skills website:
http://www.p21.org/storage/documents/docs/Intellectual_and_Pol icy_Foundations.pdf

"Manhood is about being present, not perfect." –Phil Black

we focus on the physical environment as an influencer on the participant's communication. When students become aware of the impact their surroundings have on their behavior, they can better control their behavior and be more mindful and thoughtful about their reactions. New environments and spaces can be very intimidating, and resulting insecurities can drive out negative behaviors in an effort to gain control of the situation and new environment. If we address and recognize that these uncomfortable situations are natural, participants can learn healthier ways to communicate within these new environments and make positive, lasting impressions on those they are interacting with. Additionally, participants learn to be forward thinking about new environments, considerate of those sharing that particular environment and the long-term impact their behavior within those environments might have.

Communication and Technology

- Debate their views regarding privacy and social media.
- Express why the internet and other technologies are considered public spaces.
- Determine what is considered appropriate communication over technology.
- Recognize how cyber communication can affect our futures.

In the 21st century, technology has diversified the way society communicates with one another. As technology and social media develops, younger generations grow their options for communication vehicles. As a result of technologies "newness," it is often hard to discern what the rules of engagement should be. In this session, participants are made aware of the impact of their behavior, while using technology to communicate with their peers and the outside world.

Technology also presents a long-term communication impact, as it holds the information posted, sent, and communicated for an indefinite period of time. For participants, that means that one's digital footprint could impact them at a later time in the future- even after an opinion has changed or behavior has been corrected.

Understanding Communicative Spaces

☐ Recognize the different communicative spaces (e.g. home, school, work, etc.).
☐ Discuss how our communication changes based on our environment.
☐ Identify the difference between public and private interactions.
☐ Express why our language and behavior should match our environment.

Public interactions usually happen within a public space where the possibility of others hearing the message exchange is high. On the other hand, private (termed "behind closed doors") interactions happen in a more one-on-one setting, such as face-to-face or over the phone. As settings change, our awareness regarding how we communicate in those settings should remain.

Environments have a direct impact on communication. In private situations, there is a direct and specific audience. In a public space, although there may be an intended audience, communications may reach those not intended for, due to the nature of the space and those within it.

Reputation Impact

☐ Share how individuals/schools make decisions based on facts and information, rather than emotional connections.

☐ Assess how a person's personal life and other factors can influence their business decisions.

☐ Discuss how patterns of behavior lead to lasting impressions.

☐ Identify ways to minimize poor decisions that may lead to long term consequences.

The quality of interpersonal interactions from behavior and what is communicated- is what creates a reputation for an individual. A reputation is defined as: the "beliefs or opinions that are generally held about someone or something."[27] This session addresses how others view the participants and the formation of that opinion within different instances. Understanding reputation and long term implications is important, as

---

[27] (n.d.). Retrieved September 08, 2016, from http://www.merriam-webster.com/dictionary/reputation

opportunities and disciplinary action follows the student from first impressions throughout their lifetime.

Reputations can be formed by associations, which are usually measured by the company one keeps. In this instance, reputations are transferrable. It is often assumed that students spend time with like-minded individuals. If a student is seen spending an impressionable amount of time with other students that already have preconceived opinions (from others), that student might gain that person's reputation as well- be it good or bad.

UNIT 3: THE CHOICE - SCHOOL OR PRISON?

This is a unique unit because of its format and concentrated focus. However, it is timely and directly impacts our student population. This unit of the curriculum focuses on understanding the school-to-prison pipeline. The school-to-prison pipeline describes the increasing patterns of contact that students have with the juvenile and adult criminal justice systems. These outcomes are usually a result of the practices implemented by schools, such as: zero tolerance policies and the use of police in schools. This phenomenon impacts marginalized communities, often impacting minority youth the most. As over incarceration in the United States has become a serious issue and source of disenfranchisement, addressing the school-to-prison pipeline plays an important factor to students understanding and framing their success within a school environment.

This unit is targeted early within the curriculum, mainly because of the direct implications that it has for many of our program participants. As schools continue to focus on behavior related discipline practices, including zero tolerance policies, our students are facing detrimental consequences. Due to the seriousness of these practices, we introduce the concept of the school to prison pipeline as theory and history- as an early intervention and educational tool, for our students.

"Manhood is about being present, not perfect." –Phil Black

Lesson plans to:

- Provide background on the School to Prison Pipeline
- Help participants understand the current systems landscape
- Equip students with the proper tools to advocate for themselves and their peers

Here's a list of the topics discussed in the unit:

- Prison Pipeline 1 (History)
- Buying Habits
- Prison Pipeline 2 (Today)
- Prison Pipeline (Pop Culture)
- Assessing and Selecting Your Circle

Prison Pipeline 1

- Discuss what is meant by the term "School to Prison Pipeline."
- Communicate the importance of slave labor as it relates to the US economy.
- Express how emancipation impacted business owners and individuals.

Buying Habits

- Share the primary reason businesses exist.
- Explain the concepts of products, services and a target market.

"Manhood is about being present, not perfect." –Phil Black

- Express the similarities between "buying habits" and general behavior.
- List the types of "habits" (or behaviors), one would show if he were interested in educational opportunities versus someone interested in crime.

Prison Pipeline 2 (Today) The Prison Pipeline

- Debate the intentions of the 13th amendment (to abolish slavery) and its actual language.
- Define convict leasing.
- Recognize the ways that prisons continue to make profits from prison labor and discuss other means of profit.
- Express how discussing slavery, prison, and education from an economic perspective will help to make good choices.

Prison Pipeline (Pop Culture)

- Determine the power of imagery.
- Share how the drug dealer image became a part of popular culture.
- List ways to minimize the influence media and technology has on our perception.

Assessing and Selecting Your Circle

- Identify various types of groups a person can be affiliated with.

"Manhood is about being present, not perfect." –Phil Black

- Explain how others can influence our behaviors.
- Assess our current circle of friends.
- Determine the direction (positive or negative) our circles are taking us.

Circles of influence include: friends at school, coworkers, neighbors, family members, teammates, and any other group of people, that we spend a lot of time with, especially in close-knit settings. Spending time with others can often influence our behavior. If we constantly surround ourselves with a certain group's values and perspectives- it's much easier to adapt to those thoughts, beliefs, and behaviors.

For instance, strong-willed friends can increase your self-control. When people are running low on self-control, they often seek out self-disciplined people to boost their willpower.[28]   Also, friends often bond by providing one another with the moral support needed to resist temptations. On the other hand, friends also commonly conspire together to enjoy indulgences and sometimes friends are more likely to become partners in crime as they decided to indulge together.[29]

---

[28] Shea, C. T., Davisson, E. K., & Fitzsimons, G. M. (2013). Riding Other People's Coattails: Individuals With Low Self-Control Value Self-Control in Other People. *Psychological Science*, 24(6), 1031-1036.

[29] Lowe, M. L., & Haws, K. L. (2014). (Im)moral Support: The Social Outcomes of Parallel Self-Control Decisions. J Consum Res Journal of Consumer Research, 41(2), 489-505.

"Manhood is about being present, not perfect." –Phil Black

UNIT 4: THE IMPORTANCE OF SHOWING UP (PRESENCE OVER PERFECTION)

This unit focuses on behaviors and mindsets that reflect the TMP model of being present and not perfect. In this unit, students will learn how to maintain engagement in everyday environments, even those with challenges present. Students will also learn how to fully participate as a member of a community (family, school, team), and the impact of giving- through community service.

The lessons and activities are important because challenges can often deter people from continuing involvement in positive activities and engagement with others and their communities. If we continue to reinforce strategies and the mindset of not striving for perfection, we can arm the students with behaviors to remain present within their environments.

Lesson plans to:

- Help participants establish behaviors of responsibility and commitment
- Cultivate acts of service to others within the community
- Exercise consistency and reliability in activities

Here's a list of the topics discussed in the unit:

- Be Present
- My Support

"Manhood is about being present, not perfect." –Phil Black

    ☐ Outreach Activity/Community Engagement and Service Debrief

Be Present

    ☐ List the positive qualities modeled by the character Christopher Gardner.
    ☐ Express how the character, Christopher Gardner, lived the motto and virtues of The Manhood Project.
    ☐ Explain how to begin taking on those same qualities.
    ☐ Identify people who display the positive qualities listed.

Using a biographical depiction through film- students will witness positive character traits of The Manhood Project. The students will recognize "presence" and the Five Virtues of TMP through the film's character. Even thru the character's hardships, he remains present professionally and personally. Despite being homeless, the character continues reaching his personal and work related goals. It is important that students see these positive character traits through the film's character, in addition to, their TMP facilitator and guest speakers.

Here, being present means showing up for responsibilities that are required at that moment while remaining mindful of the goal to become better. Being present is giving full awareness to the "here and now." As the motto reflects, focus is not on perfection, but more about one's presence. Hardships will come and

"Manhood is about being present, not perfect." –Phil Black

84

perfection is unattainable, but being the very best one can be at that time, with the right tools and foundation, is all that's necessary.

<u>My Support</u>

- ☐ Identify the individuals who helped in your growth and development.
- ☐ Discuss the impact others have made in our lives.
- ☐ Share the benefits of helping others in need.
- ☐ Determine what it means to be "an active citizen" within our society.

Support systems are a group of people who offer help or encouragement through different resources. Resources come in the form of: emotional, spiritual, financial, or guidance. It is important that the participants identify those within their support system and recognize the ways they are supported.

Identifying support systems also helps shape how participants can be a support system to others. Having a support system has many positive benefits, such as higher levels of well-being, better coping skills, as well a longer and healthier life. Studies have also shown that social support can reduce depression and anxiety. By providing support to others (friends, family, neighbors, classmates, etc.)- a sense of belonging, trust, and responsibility can result.

"Manhood is about being present, not perfect." –Phil Black

Outreach Activity/Community Engagement and Service Debrief

- Share the aspects of service enjoyed most.
- Discuss what lessons were learned, by helping others.
- Express ways to improve the experience.

Students will put into action the lessons they've learned in this unit about being present and supportive of their community. Students will also exhibit positive behaviors through a community engagement activity. It is important that students can practice their new skill sets and receive support, guidance, and feedback during the process. Through sharing experiences with one another, students can express the impact that the activity had and continue to build community togetherness as a cohort.

"Manhood is about being present, not perfect." –Phil Black

UNIT 5: LIVING THE FIVE VIRTUES

The Manhood Project is built upon the Five Virtues of manhood that reflect behavior showing high moral standards. Theses virtues: love, respect, courage, provision, and protection- combine into a foundation of standards that will guide intentions and motivations.

At this point in the curriculum, the lessons will address not only specific behavior and awareness, but setting everyday principles of intention. These intentions require emotional intelligence that should have been ascertained throughout the previous lessons.

Lesson plans to:

- Explore TMP's Five Virtues of Manhood
- Understand the importance of the Five Virtues
- Learn how to implement the Five Virtues in daily life practice

Here's a list of the topics discussed within the unit:

- Establishing a Moral Code
- Love
- Respect
- Courage, Provision, and Protection

"Manhood is about being present, not perfect." –Phil Black

Establishing a Moral Code

- Define Moral Code.
- Determine how we are currently being guided in our lives outside of the program.
- Recognize the importance of being properly guided by others (through mentorship), and ourselves (internally through our moral code).
- Identify the Five Virtues as a framework for establishing a personal moral code.

A moral code is a written, formal, and consistent set of rules prescribing righteous behavior, accepted by a person or by a group of people.[30] For TMP, the moral code is the Five Virtues framework to guide thinking and behavior. Having a guide or code to live by is important in daily habits, behaviors, and decision-making. It is important for the participants to recognize the influence of others in establishing an informal, and possibly not recognized current code, and the impact it has on daily life outcomes.

By being mindful about moral codes, and understanding how the Five Virtues can help frame morality, the participants can integrate their own expectations of behavior and guidance. This allows the participants power over their lives and guides their decision-making long term.

---

[30] Moral-code dictionary definition | moral-code defined. (n.d.). Retrieved September 08, 2016, from http://www.yourdictionary.com/moral-code#P7vQTL51ZQTl7STu.99

"Manhood is about being present, not perfect." –Phil Black

As a larger group, the Five Virtues as a moral code is a series of agreements to which a person has subscribed to guarantee the survival of a group-manhood.

LOVE

- Define love for self, family, others and community.
- Communicate the importance of loving one's self first.
- Identify ways to demonstrate love.
- Recognize how to love others without losing love for self.

As a virtue of The Manhood Project model- love is reflected in many forms. In the lessons, love is taught as both: affection one can show himself and outward care towards others. Self-love is defined as regard for one's own well-being and happiness, in a desirable and positive way. Here, we present it as a necessary foundation in order to love others. Self-love must be exhibited before any other kind of love, as it is the most intimate and vulnerable. Self-love is the most forgiving and most accepting.

Outward love can be exhibited in many ways. Outward love shows care and concern for others, and incorporates the same forgiveness and acceptance that self-love models. When love for self comes first, outward love is then displayed and reflected.

To balance both inward and outward love, students should understand that love requires not expecting something in return from others. In fact, because of self-love, they'll have all they love that is necessary for them to live a life of joy and fulfillment. The balance lies in everyone being who they are- naturally.

RESPECT
- Discuss what it means to be respected.
- Share ways to earn respect.
- Express what it means to be both disrespected and disrespectful.
- Communicate how showing respect towards others can increase the likelihood of receiving respect in return.

Unlike love, which is unconditional, respect is an admiration for someone or something, elicited by their abilities, qualities, or achievements. Respect is a way of treating or thinking about something or someone. Respect is an earned trait that we solicit for ourselves and give unto others.

Respect is a virtue of The Manhood Project that helps direct participants' long-term paths and behaviors- by driving motivations for traits to earn respect from others.

COURAGE, PROVISION, AND PROTECTION
- Define courage and what it means to be courageous.

"Manhood is about being present, not perfect." –Phil Black

Courage is defined as mental or moral strength to venture, persevere, and withstand danger, fear, or difficulty. To be courageous is to have a quality of mind to face fears and take action- despite the perceived challenges. For The Manhood Project, the participants learn to be courageous, by understanding that they can conquer any challenges or obstacles with faith and the sheer determination and will to succeed. The participants also learn that courage is faith in being successful.

- Recognize the importance of building a foundation for the future.
- Communicate ways to prepare for a strong family.

Being forward in thinking helps participants set goals that are practical and goal-oriented. When participants build a foundation for their future, they understand that their actions and behaviors will now directly impact future outcomes. In that sense of manhood, the concept of preparing for the future is one that reflects care and provision of self, family, and community.

- Explain why protecting those that are unable to protect themselves is a vital part of being a man.

Protection is a virtue of manhood that teaches how to safeguard others from harm. The concept of harm does not have to be physical. Instead, protection could also include emotional and spiritual harm as well. With wisdom, knowledge, and personal

"Manhood is about being present, not perfect." –Phil Black

experience, one can protect those that are more vulnerable or who have a lack of resources to protect themselves.

UNIT 6: DISCIPLINE, SELF-GUIDANCE, AND LEADERSHIP

The final unit concludes by reiterating lessons and experiences throughout the curriculum for everyday life application. This unit puts into action, the important tools for the students to manifest the Five Virtues and self-awareness taught by the program in the previous five units.

The curriculum closes with these lessons, so that students can have a basic roadmap of understanding how everything they've studied can be incorporated into their lives from the day they finish TMP through adulthood.

Lesson plans to:

☐ Give students tools to execute positive behavioral change
☐ Provide methods for students to support and encourage others to exhibit positive behaviors
☐ Create long-lasting positive and impactful behavior

Here's a list of the topics discussed within the unit:

☐ My Journey
☐ Leadership
☐ Motivation 101
☐ Inspiration

"Manhood is about being present, not perfect." –Phil Black

93

<u>My Journey</u>

Discuss positive changes and progress made since beginning the program.

- Share personal stories of praise from others that have noticed growth and improvement.
- Set at least one goal to be accomplished after the program has concluded.

Positive evaluation and sharing of achievements both privately and as a group- has a tremendous impact on youth behavior. Not only does it create a positive learning environment, it reinforces positive behaviors and creates a positive sense of community. Positive affirmations and reflections of growth should be recognized from those within the program and within the participants lives outside of the program- including (but not limited to) teachers, school staff, family, and friends.

It is also important that students themselves recognize their own changes and reflect on how they feel. By setting goals for themselves once the program is complete they reiterate the lessons as a part of their new identity and behavior, holding themselves accountable to continue positive growth and change.

<u>Leadership</u>

- Define leadership.
- Identify examples of positive and poor leaders.
- Determine what type of leader they want to be.

"Manhood is about being present, not perfect." –Phil Black

☐ Express the steps needed to take on the characteristics of a leader.

Identifying traits of leadership helps the student recognize leadership traits they'd like to exhibit and mimic to lead to positive life outcomes. An important aspect of TMP's concept of manhood- leadership is defined as the action of leading a group of people or community. A leader guides, influences, and shows others the right direction to follow.

As the program continues, participants should start to fully understand their own personal experiences and apply them to the new experiences they'd like to forge from the concepts that they've learned.

Motivation 101

☐ Reflect on the people and events (past or present) that are most important to them and the impact that those people have made in your life.
☐ Communicate the difference between Motivation and Inspiration.
☐ Develop a why statement.
☐ Recognize how to use their "why" as motivation to excel.

Here, motivation is a set of goals resulting from a particular action. Motivation may provide benchmarks or rewards, for behavior or specific activities. In most instances, the motivation should be positive but often

"Manhood is about being present, not perfect." –Phil Black

it provides a path for a desired outcome. In essence, motivation is the desire to do things.

Identifying and creating motivation allows participants to understand why they've chosen specific activities and what goals they'd like to achieve.

Inspiration

- Share who or what inspires them.
- Create a vision board.
- Communicate how they will use what they have learned to inspire others.

To inspire is to create a positive feeling within a person that ignites positive and impactful behavior. Furthermore, inspiration is a reflection of one's spirit with the end goal of fulfillment. As the students reflect on their own inspirations, they also develop plans on how to inspire others. This is important because the students are now fully aware of their behavior and the ways that they can personally impact others. This gives a sense of power and understanding to do good work throughout their community. Throughout the program, participants work on creating their best self and we (as facilitators) focus the attention on the student as an individual and remind them of the impact that they have on others- including the world around them.

"Manhood is about being present, not perfect." –Phil Black

OTHER SESSIONS

"Manhood is about being present, not perfect." –Phil Black

GUEST SPEAKER

The Manhood Project invites guest speakers to interact with the students regularly throughout every unit as a direct implementation of the exposure module in our four-part approach to leadership development. Guest speakers offer a different perspective from regular facilitators, often enhancing the lessons throughout the program. Having guest speakers gives real world application to the material you are teaching. Additionally, the students are also creating another mentoring relationship, while reaping the benefits of additional adult attention and positive-reinforcement. The speakers also get a chance to contribute to the program and the community by their participation.[31]

---

[31] Wortmann. (1992). An invitation to learning: Guest speakers in the classroom. *The Science Teacher*, 59, 19-22.

"Manhood is about being present, not perfect." –Phil Black

STUDENT ONE-ON-ONES AND SELF CARE DAY

Initial Meeting:

- Share brief information about yourself as the facilitator/coach of the program and why you have chosen to do this work.
- Gain basic information from the student about themselves and gauge their level of understanding around coaching and the program in general.
- Determine how having a coach and participating in the program may benefit the student from their own perspective.
- Highlight desired outcomes and expectations, while receiving the expectations of the student.

Ongoing Meetings:

- Assess students overall feelings about the program and his participation.
- Evaluate student's progress towards goals.
- Set goals for next meeting.

One-on-One's and Self Care allow for students and facilitators to connect as mentee and mentor in a private setting. Cultivating this personal relationship is important to both parties as it allows an intimate relationship to build. These interactions allow the mentor and facilitator to specifically review the participant's needs, by getting to know one another personally, developing a rapport, and setting specific goals outside of the group.

"Manhood is about being present, not perfect." –Phil Black

These sessions are also a great way for the facilitator to receive detailed feedback about the program, the included sessions, so that they can make any changes deemed necessary.

Assessment, Recognition, and Reflection

- Identify the most impactful aspects of the Unit.
- Share any changes made since the first session.
- Recognize students that have made improvements.

Student recognition is the primary way The Manhood Project motivates and encourages students through assessment and evaluation. While self-comparison has negative effects on behavioral outcomes and creates a competitive environment, recognizing the student's effort creates feelings of belonging, active engagement, self-regulation, interests in activities, and overall focus on personal effort and learning.[32]

- Set goals for the next unit.

Continuously setting goals for achievement and learning prepares the participants for what to expect when the next unit begins. After recognizing the goals met during the current unit, setting goals now allows students to shape continued goals with a positive mindset. Specifically, the positive mindset reminds

---

[32] Ames, C. (1992). Classrooms: Goals, structures, and student motivation. *Journal of Educational Psychology,* 84(3), 261-271.

"Manhood is about being present, not perfect." –Phil Black

them that the goals throughout the program are achievable individually and as a group.

"Manhood is about being present, not perfect." –Phil Black

LOCKER ROOM

In recognition of the need for flexibility in programming, specifically regarding the individual needs of a broad audience of participants, we've designed a session called "Locker Room." As the name suggests, Locker Room is a time completely devoted to discussing personal challenges, exploring random ideas, current events or just to offer a mental break from the structured/academic format of the program. It is intended to provide a safe space for students to receive advice from you (as their facilitator/coach) and peers- a time to simply team build.

As it is addressed in Highlights and Do-Overs, the space to address challenges creates a safe space for students to build community and confidence, as well as, show new approaches to perception and behavior learned through past sessions.

The activities for Locker Room foster discussion among the participants and allows for participants to lead the discussion with guidance- if necessary, from the facilitator. Activities can include:

- ☐ Real Talk
- ☐ Round Table Talks
- ☐ Current Events
- ☐ Snap Debates

"Manhood is about being present, not perfect." –Phil Black

IN CONCLUSION

The Manhood Project Curriculum, and these Principles of the Project, were inspired by my personal life experiences, built and developed using solid research, scientific strategies, and proven methodologies. The goal for this project was to provide you with the same tools and information that is responsible for my success as a coach and mentor. I truly believe that the more informed we are collectively, the better off we are to equip our youth with the love and guidance needed for a healthy life.

I encourage you to continue beyond these pages. Read more on ADDIE and Maslow's Hierarchy. If you have not done so, become certified as a youth coach. The Youth Coaching Institute I've referred to, with Dr. Leah Mazolla, is a great program that will prepare you with a number of skills applicable to many fields (teaching, counseling, management, etc.). Learn more about Clover through the PEAR Institute. Dr. Noam's model provides a common language and relative strategies that are easy to apply and will enhance your understanding and ability to engage youth. Lastly, should you commit to being the difference within your community, make sure you purchase the TMP Curriculum Manual. Not only will it give you enough material to host at least one weekly session for a full calendar year, it will also aide in building your skillset as a facilitator. These tools are exceptional and will enhance your effectiveness. You deserve to be the best that you can, and our children deserve the best that you have to offer.

"Manhood is about being present, not perfect." –Phil Black

You don't have to be perfect, but you do have to be present.

Made in the USA
Monee, IL
31 January 2024

52104567R00063